tea

the perfect brew

tea

the perfect brew

Jane Campsie

photography Fleur Olby

MURDOCH
B O O K S

contents

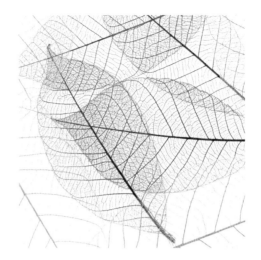

a taste
for tea 6

health
cup 20

tea
essentials 38

natural
infusions 56

tisanes
and tonics 80

tea
directory 92

index 94

the tea ritual · tea past and present · cultural traditions · a global cup

a taste for tea

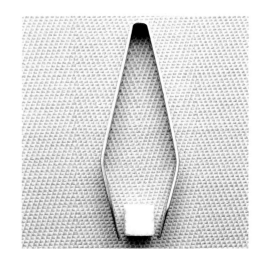

the tea
ritual

More than just a drink, tea is a sign of good taste, a mark of conviviality, a gesture of friendship, a comfort for the bereaved, an excuse to unite, a spiritual quest as well as a calming, healthy experience. Appreciated all over the world for years, drinking tea is an integral part of daily life in many cultures. In China, it represents meditation and communication and, in the Japanese tea ceremony, each sip is an initiation.

Rediscover the art of making the perfect brew and savour the taste of tea. Do not rush the ritual, but make the time to appreciate the moment and make it a sensory experience. Use tactile contemporary earthenware that appeals both to the eye and to the touch. Invest in quality tea with a rich aroma and flavoursome taste, to satisfy your sense of smell and get your taste buds going. Reap its health benefits and use tea as a tonic for the mind and body. Make tea a social affair and invite friends over. Most importantly: have fun. Delve into the future and read your tea leaves. Indulge in cakes with afternoon tea. Enjoy the experience and relish the moment.

The natural, comforting and wholesome appeal of tea makes it one of the world's most popular beverages. However, many of us are still not aware of the array of teas on offer or the health benefits of this plant. Research has shown that people who drink one or more cups of tea every day are only half as likely to suffer a heart attack as those who do not drink tea at all. Tea is also a great preventative tonic for tooth decay, cancer and fluid retention. The association of tea with health is well established, especially since tea was discovered so long ago. An ancient legend has it that tea was first discovered when the leaves from a wild tea bush were blown into a pan of boiling water belonging to the Chinese Emperor Shen Nung. He was a scholar and herbalist who only drank boiled water for health and hygiene purposes. After sampling his new-found brew, he took to the taste and tea was 'discovered' in 2737 BC.

tea past
and present

Gradually, news spread of the acquired taste for tea. By AD 450, tea was perceived as the elixir of immortality and was being consumed for its many health benefits. A century later, a Buddhist monk, returning to his native Japan, brought a tea plant back with him, and word quickly spread of the new brew. In AD 780, the poet Lu Yu wrote the great *Ch'a Ching, Book of Tea*. As the world discovered tea, it caught on not merely as a medicinal cup, but was being sipped to satisfy the taste buds.

tea smuggling

When tea finally took off in the West in the 18th and 19th centuries, it was at first a highly prized commodity, reserved for the elite. However, in Britain, tea became an integral part of British society at all levels, and was both a working class cup and an aristocratic affair − the rich sipping the best grades of tea and the poor the cheap ones. By the middle of the 18th century, tea became an indulgence as taxes reached extortionate limits. This left a bad taste in the mouth of the tea-loving nation and, in order to evade taxes, the smuggling of tea became big business. However, even though tea was soon readily available on the black market, it was still expensive. The cost of a pound of tea equated to one third of the average weekly wage at the time. As the demand for tea rose, the finest leaves were blended with willow, elder and aloe leaves to go further and disconcerting tea drinkers even mixed tea with ash leaf and sheep dung. Tea leaves were used, dried out and reused. By 1784, a law was passed to slash taxes to try to put a stop to smuggling. In 1875, the English Food and Drug Act imposed heavy fines and imprisonment on those caught smuggling tea. Above-board tea trading became favourable and business boomed. However, just like any other tradable goods, tea went in and out of fashion.

wartime rationing

During the First World War, tea imports suffered and tea soon re-emerged on the black market. However, rationing was introduced and the Government fixed prices. During the Second World War, tea became such a national morale booster that it was dispatched to 500 destinations so the country's supplies would not be destroyed by air raids. Tea drinking reached new heights during the war, offering comfort and salvation to both the armed forces and civilians.

cultural traditions

Every country has its own way of brewing and serving tea. In Tibet, salty green tea is blended with goat's milk or yak butter. In Japan, drinking tea is a ritual and the tea ceremony, known as *cha-no-yu*, can last up to 4 hours, and as many as 24 utensils are used.

japanese tea ritual   The Japanese tea ceremony stems from Zen religion as the first tea masters were priests, who fervently believed that enlightenment could only be reached through Zen meditation. The tea ceremony was used as a means of disciplining the mind. Tea schools, which are still running in Japan today, were set up to teach the etiquette and art of tea making. The Japanese tea ceremony is based on five main principles: hygiene, harmony, humility, reverence and peace. The first principle, hygiene, embodies a form of respect and doing things well. Harmony symbolizes unity between its participants. Humility, which is represented by a low doorway to be entered, teaches the evils of egotism. Reverence implies total respect for one another as well as for the tea ritual. Finally, the last principle, peace, reflects self-discipline.

Each tea ceremony is a unique experience. It starts after the traditional Japanese meal, when the guests are seated on tatami mats, on the floor, in a tea room. The colour of the kimonos, the flowers, decorative scrolls, the type of bowls, the utensils and the setting all play an important role. Large china bowls are used to drink powdered green tea, known as Matcha. It is mixed with water heated to 85°C (185°F), then lightly whisked with a *chasen* (bamboo whisk) to make a rich, frothy liquor, which is presented to the guest, and turned three times before it is drunk in three sips. The bowl is then wiped with a silk cloth three times, refilled and passed on to the next guest.

the chinese brew   In China, a single cup of tea is brewed by infusing the leaves in a *guywan* (covered cup and saucer). The leaves are placed in the cup. Then boiled water, which has been left to cool slightly, is added and the lid is placed on the cup so the leaves can infuse. The tea is sipped, using the lid as a strainer to keep the leaves in the cup. The Chinese assert that the second infusion is the best. It is also common practice to use a small teapot and handleless cups or glasses.

turkish tradition   Contrary to popular belief, the Turks drink more tea than coffee and, in most households, there is always a pot of tea on the fire. They serve it topped up with boiling water. The art of tea making is so important in Turkey that all brides-to-be must be competent in *demilikacay* (preparing tea).

moroccan cup   The Moroccans highly favour fragrant mint tea, which is brewed in ornate silver teapots and served in decorative tea glasses. Fresh mint leaves are infused in boiling water and served with sugar in order to dissipate the bitter taste. It has also become customary to mix green tea with fresh mint leaves as a means of obtaining a smoother, more flavoursome cup. The art of serving Moroccan tea lies in pouring it high above the glasses to create froth on the surface.

tibetan brew   In Tibet, *tsampa* time is most sacred, so much care and attention is taken to brew even a small amount of green brick tea. The tea is infused, then strained and mixed with salt and either goat's milk or yak butter. It is served with cake made from corn or barley, known as *tsamba*.

indian spice   The traditional approach in India is to create a spicy brew, blending black tea with milk and spices such as cloves, cardamoms and cinnamon offset with lots of sugar. It is served on the streets in clay cups that are smashed after drinking.

egyptian way   Contrary to widespread beliefs, Islamic law does not forbid drinking black tea on the grounds that it is fermented. In Egypt, Pakistan and Saudi Arabia, black tea from India or Ceylon is favoured. Tea is served strong and very sweet, but without milk.

south american cup   South Americans favour Mate tea, which is a blend of young leaves and shoots. This tea is both infused and served in a hollowed-out, pear-shaped gourd known as a *calabaza*. It is drunk with a metal or wooden *bombilla* tea straw, to ensure that no infusing matter is ingested.

russian practice   The Russians prefer drinking green and black tea, without milk. To best savour the taste of strong, bitter tea, a spoonful of fruit jam (jelly) is placed on the tongue, merging the sweet and bitter tastes.

tea customs

Tea is surrounded with rituals. Throughout history, it has been used to reveal the future, as well as an indicator of social backgrounds, personal ambitions and amorous pursuits.

making names

Tea was originally referred to as *tcha*, *cha*, *tay* or *tee*. The English version, 'tea' originated from the Chinese word *te*, which is pronounced 'tay'. This may appear somewhat confusing, but 'tea' is in fact a universal word that sounds very similar in most dialects. You drink *thé* in France, *tee* in Finland, *ta* in Korea, *chay* in Turkey, *chai* in Russia. If you speak Cantonese, you will drink *ch'a*, but if your language is Mandarin, you drink *cha*. This way, tea lovers will never find it difficult to get hold of their favourite brew wherever they are. The word 'tea' has also had many other meanings in slang throughout history. In the 1900s in England, a 'tea-leaf' was a thief, to 'smash the teapot' meant to break a pledge of abstinence and a 'tea bottle' was the name given to an old maid who loved her pots of tea.

tea breaks

The tradition of having a tea break has been in place for over 200 years in Britain. It originated when employers decided to offer their workers a mid-morning cup and an afternoon break to compensate for the long working hours. Between 1741 and 1820, employers tried to put a stop to tea breaks, maintaining that it was making workers lazy. After much protesting, workers retained their right to having a tea break. When trade unions were introduced, workforces became legally entitled to a tea break. A tea break is an excellent opportunity to replenish energy levels and refuel the body. The caffeine found in tea acts as a natural pick-me-up and added sugar will also give you an extra boost. Take the time to savour your cup at work, especially when you are feeling stressed – it will make a difference.

reading matter

Tassiology, or teacup reading, with its roots in folklore and ideology, reveals what the future holds. The reader interprets shapes and forms made by the tea leaves. Without using a strainer, pour tea into a cup. Allow the person whose fortune is to be revealed to drink the tea, leaving a small amount of tea in the cup. Swirl the liquid around three times clockwise and then three times anti-clockwise. Pour the liquid away and examine how the leaves have collected in the cup. If three small leaves appear close to a large leaf, this symbolizes a man. Two small leaves next to a smaller leaf suggest a woman, whereas small leaves forming a triangular shape represent a child. A key shape implies secrets, and if your tea leaves collect in a heart shape, then love is on your doorstep.

hidden meanings

During the 19th century, tea played an important role in high society. How tea was served and brewed was important, and had a lot to answer for. It helped differentiate one social class from the other. It also served as a mirror to one's intentions. For instance, those who were keen to show their affections to loved ones used tea to help them in their seduction parade. The subtle act of pouring tea in such a way that froth formed on the surface of the cup was a tip-off that a love letter or a kiss was on its way. If you want to give your love life a boost, try sipping ginseng tea three to four times a day. Ginseng is a great libido boost for women, and has therefore been used for years to stimulate powers of seduction. Make sure to limit your intake though, as excessive doses of ginseng can lead to hypertension.

a global cup

In addition to its comforting appeal and flavoursome taste, tea has been drunk for centuries as a means of boosting both the mind and body in a natural way.

wise words

According to an ancient Japanese proverb, 'if a man has no tea in him, he is incapable of understanding truth and beauty'. George Orwell once noted that 'you feel wiser, braver and more optimistic after a cup of it'. According to an ancient Chinese legend, each day virgins with sweet-scented breath would pick both a leaf and bud from each bush for the emperors to brew.

mental boost

For years now, tea has been recognized for its ability to improve both alertness and clarity of mind. Buddhist monks are the ones who introduced the tea plant to their homeland Japan. They claimed that an infusion of leaves helped them to stay awake and focus during their prolonged periods of meditation. So, when you are feeling tired, opt for a revitalizing cup of tea.

contemplation cup

For centuries, those in the know have been turning to tea to treat a pounding head. Try not to reach immediately for conventional painkillers. Instead, sit down, relax and have a cup of green tea. Green tea contains a small amount of caffeine that will help get rid of a headache and is a much better option than taking two painkillers, which contain an average of 60mg of caffeine.

refreshing tonic

Iced tea is a refreshing drink that works as a pick-me-up when the heat is on. It was invented in 1904, when tea dealer Richard Blechyuden was in much despair. Sweltering heat was deterring people from sampling his hot tea at a tea fair, so he improvized and served it with ice cubes. Today, iced tea is very popular, and North Americans actually drink more iced tea than hot tea.

weighing in

Green tea has been the national drink in Japan for many years now, and this could explain why as a nation, they have such svelte figures. Apart from all the rituals and the abundance of health benefits that are associated with green tea, drinking this refreshing brew can prevent piling on the pounds as well. New research shows that extracts in green tea speed up fat oxidation.

liberating brew

Apart from its appealing taste and many health benefits, tea also helped in the fight for women's emancipation. In Britain, the manageress of a bread shop persuaded the management to allow her to serve tea and light snacks to customers. The idea took off, tea rooms soon opened everywhere and eventually, women were allowed to meet unchaperoned from 1864.

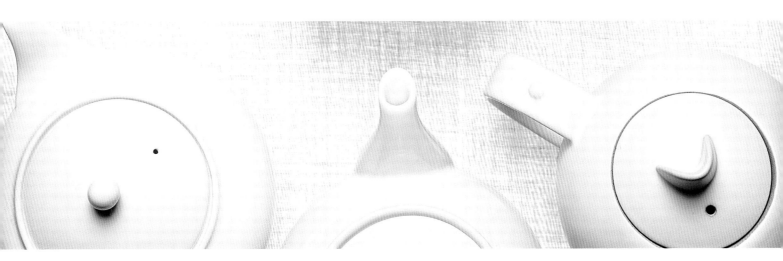

drink to your health · a pot full of potential · beauty boost · tea production · types of tea

health cup

drink to
your health

Tea is a healing infusion and for centuries, this curative cup has been served up to treat many ailments. The Ancient Greeks used to drink tea to treat colds and flu, and it was also traditionally used to treat diarrhoeal diseases such as cholera, leaving its antibacterial and astringent properties to fight infections. The Chinese have been drinking tea for years to aid digestion and improve mental and physical performance.

Experts maintain that if non-tea drinkers were to take to tea and have just one cup of black or green tea each day, it would make a significant impact on their overall health, helping them to protect their body against many prevalent diseases. If you are not keen on either black or green tea, try jasmine, which is a flavoured green tea. The good news for tea aficionados is that you cannot get too much of a good thing, unless your daily intake exceeds 10 to 15 cups. Tea is both calorie-free and fat-free if served without milk or sugar. It is also low in sodium and contains vital traces of proteins, carbohydrates, amino acids and lipids. The average daily intake of tea in the UK tops 3.5 cups, which provides 16 per cent of the daily requirement of calcium, 10 per cent of our folic acid and zinc requirements, 9 per cent of the required daily intake of vitamin B1, 25 per cent of the daily intake of vitamin B2 and 6 per cent of the daily requirement for vitamin B6. Tea also contains manganese, which is vital for the growth and development of healthy bones; potassium, which is needed to regulate fluid levels within the body; and fluoride, which helps prevent tooth and gum problems. Black and green tea both rate high on the health list, but green tea actually contains a greater level of antioxidants, five times higher than that of black tea. Adding either a little milk or a slice of lemon will not inhibit the health properties of tea but nonetheless, if the tea becomes either too strong, too sugary or too salty, it could possibly neutralize some of the health benefits of your cup.

a pot full
of potential

The rich source of antioxidants, known as flavonoids, found in black and green tea is the key health property of tea. Antioxidants help fight against damaging free radicals, the rogue molecules that set off a slow chain reaction within the body to destroy cells and degenerate the body's organs. Free radicals are also responsible for premature ageing, weakening the immune system and the onset of many chronic diseases, including heart disease and cancer.

One cup of tea fuels the body with around 200mg of flavonoids, which are released in the first minute of brewing. Research shows that sipping three cups of tea daily over a two-week period increases the concentration of flavonoids in the blood by 25 per cent.

healthy heart Tea lovers will be pleased to hear that tea is excellent for the heart. Research has proved that the drop in both blood cholesterol levels and blood pressure is proportional to the increase in tea consumption. This is due to the flavonoids, which have the benefit of reducing blood clotting as well as the deposit of cholesterol in the blood vessels.

tooth tactics Tea also helps to keep teeth and gums healthy, as it fuels the teeth with fluoride, which prevents tooth decay and gum disease. The tea plant absorbs fluoride from the soil as it grows, and stores it in its leaves. A cup of tea yields between 0.3 and 0.5mg of fluoride. Tea also stimulates saliva production which, in turn, stops plaque from forming. Research confirms that just one cup of tea each day can reduce the risk of tooth decay. The only drawback is that it can stain the teeth, but regular brushing should prevent this. However, if strong discolouration occurs, you should see an oral hygienist or try using a whitening toothpaste.

healthy measures Researchers are also making headway with studies looking at tea's ability to help in the fight against cancer, revealing that tea plays a significant role against the development of pancreatic and prostate cancer. Tea also ranks high in its ability to inhibit the growth of some tumour cells. Studies have shown that men who drink up to three cups of tea each day may reduce their risk of developing prostate cancer compared to non-tea drinkers.

beauty boost

Apart from quenching thirst and fuelling our health from within, tea has also been used for centuries for its beautifying benefits. The rich source of antioxidants in green tea explains why it is used in many sunscreens, anti-ageing preparations, facial toners, shampoos and anti-cellulite preparations. The Japanese have always concocted teas that maintain a radiant complexion from within, and used tea to topically treat their skin and condition their hair. During the Second World War, when stockings were in short supply, women used cold tea to stain their legs in an attempt to mimic the flesh-coloured tones of stockings.

bathing ritual In order to reap even more benefits from tea, take to the bathtub and throw a couple of tea bags into running water to infuse. Green tea will both protect and preserve the skin. Peppermint tea creates an invigorating infusion, while the aromatic vapours will help clear nasal congestion in the winter. The comforting aroma of both chamomile tea and lavender infusions will prove relaxing, calm overactive minds and provide the perfect antidote for treating skins prone to irritation and disorders such as

eczema or psoriasis. A tepid chamomile infusion is ideal for children and babies whose skin reacts to most commercial detergents.

preserving beauty If your feet are tired and weary, lace a bowl of boiled water with peppermint or ginseng tea bags. Place some marbles in the bottom of the bowl. Then place your feet in the bowl and gently run your feet over the marbles to relax and revive them. Many herbal infusions are ideal as final rinses after shampooing hair. Rosemary will make hair lustrous and healthy looking, while an infusion of chamomile flowers will enhance the natural colouring of blondes. If culinary smells linger after preparing food, try pouring cold tea over your hands.

cold cure Cold tea bags come into their own to treat many ailments. Cold chamomile tea bags can be squeezed out and placed over the eyelids to relieve tiredness and under-eye puffiness. For nipples sore from breastfeeding, place a used black tea bag on them to soothe. To prevent swelling after injections, place a used green tea bag on the skin. Soothe a black eye by placing a warm black tea bag on it.

the tea plant

Tea is produced from the *camellia sinensis*, an evergreen plant that thrives in the hot, humid climates of mainly China, Tibet and Japan. This bush, which is part of the camellia family, produces shiny leaves that are 5 centimetres (2 inches) long and small, white flowers, and flourishes for up to 100 years. Other varieties of tea-producing plants include the *camellia assamica*, which is classified as a tree rather than a bush, and produces leaves that can be 15 to 35 centimetres (6 to 14 inches) long for up to 40 years. The *camellia assamica* subspecies *lasiocalyx* is another tree used in the production of hybrids.

Climate, soil condition, altitude, when and how the tea is picked and processed, the blend used, as well as packaging and storage will all determine the end result. Research shows that tea grown at high altitude in humid conditions yields a finer-quality tea. When tea leaves are picked, they contain amino acids, carbohydrates, minerals, caffeine and polyphenolic compounds, along with a high percentage of water. All of these contribute to the overall taste and flavour of tea but, as the leaves are processed, the water content reduces to develop different types of tea.

tea harvest The leaves of the tea plant are either hand-picked or harvested by machine. In the past, when tea bushes reached great heights, monkeys were trained to climb the bushes and pick the leaves. The first flush of tea is collected in early spring and the second flush in late spring. Both Darjeeling and Assam varieties are well known for their first- and second-flush teas. Once picked, the leaves are either left to wither and dry in the sun, steamed and rolled, or they are twisted and then fired. Different tea-processing methods produce different teas.

famous blends Japan, China and Indonesia were the main producers of tea on a commercial scale until the early 19th century. Today, over 25 countries grow tea, generating over 2,600,000 tonnes (2,340,000 tons) every year. Teas can be defined by their origin or by their blends. India is known for Assam, Darjeeling and Nilgiri teas, whereas Sri Lanka is renowned for its Ceylon blends and Dimbula, Nuwara Eliya and Uva teas. China is famed for its green, Oolong, white and flavoured teas while Indonesia is recognized for producing light, flavourful, brightly coloured teas.

tea origins

chinese teas   Green tea is the favoured drink in China, but vast quantities of Oolong, Pouchong and black tea are produced for export. Keemun is a well-known black China tea, with an orchid aroma and a mild, sweet flavour, producing a red liquor. It makes an ideal evening drink, and is also used as a base for many scented blends. China is also known for its Pu-erh (or Puer) tea. This digestive aid is made from the leaves of the subspecies of the tea plant *camellia sinensis assamica*. They are fermented twice and stored to mature.

indian teas   After China, India produces more tea than any other country. The three main growing areas are Assam, Darjeeling and Nilgiri. Tea grown in Assam has a strong, malty taste, making it a perfect breakfast tea, as it can tolerate a little milk. Darjeeling tea, a rare and premium black tea, is produced in the small town of Darjeeling, in the foothills of the Himalayas. It is a light-coloured, delicately scented tea that tastes of green grapes.

japanese teas   In Japan, the only type of tea grown is green tea. The most common varieties are Sencha and Bancha, but Gyokuro is the best quality. The bushes are sheltered from the sun prior to picking for 21 days, to create a sweeter, more intense flavoured tea. Ground Gyokuro leaves are used to create the powdered green tea, known as Matcha Uji (froth of liquid jade), a jade-green liquor great for iced tea, sauces and sherbets. Also popular is Genmaicha (Japanese rice), which is a blend of Bancha, corn and toasted rice. Houjicha, a roasted version of Sencha or Bancha is a light, sweet-tasting brew that is perfect to accompany light meals.

ceylon teas   Sri Lanka, formerly known as Ceylon, grows tea mainly in Uva, Nuwara Eliya and Dimbula. Uva tea is fragrant and has an intense taste. Nuwara Eliya tea is light in colour, with a very distinctive aroma and taste. Dimbula tea is light in both flavour and aroma.

organic teas   The production of organic tea has become increasingly popular, despite a major drawback: it takes three years of tests and inspections for a tea plantation to be certified as organic. With organic farming methods, tea leaves are not subjected to any chemical fertilizers, pesticides or herbicides.

tea
production

tea grades
Tea leaves are graded into different-sized pieces of leaf, as the size relates to how long the tea will take to infuse. The smaller the piece, the quicker it will infuse. Tea dust refers to the smallest leaf particles, which are usually used in tea bags as they infuse the quickest. Tea fannings are the small, grainy particles of the leaf that are sifted out of better-grade teas. These still make a good-quality, flavoursome brew. The finest quality teas are made up of whole-leaf or broken-leaf tea, which consists of the larger pieces of tea leaves. Professional tea graders use a complex language to classify tea grades and differentiate between the different types and qualities of tea.

tea tasting
Tasters are responsible for checking the quality of teas and describing them in preparation for commercial sales. They are expected to ensure that the quality is consistent and identify what tea companies should be buying from which producers. Appearance, aroma and colour are taken into consideration. An experienced taster will be able to identify everything from the time the leaf was picked to the height of the tea bush.

blended teas
Certain types of tea are not blended, while others are mixed to create more palatable brews. English Breakfast tea, which is a blend of Assam tea (for colour and strength), Ceylon tea (for flavour) and African tea (for depth), is the perfect accompaniment for a hearty breakfast. Irish blends are usually a blend of Assam and African teas, which have a stronger, hearty flavour. Afternoon tea blends are often a mix of Darjeeling, Ceylon and China black teas such as Keemun. There are no set rules to create your own, personal tea blends, so simply try mixing together different types of tea until you come up with your preferred taste.

flavoured teas
Tea can be flavoured with spices, herbs, flowers, berries and even onions. The most popular flavoured teas are mixed from black, Pouchong or green teas. In China, teas are laced with jasmine flowers, honeysuckle, rose petals, osmanthus and orchids. In India, black tea is flavoured with cardamoms and spices. Innovative flavourings are now readily available, with tea tastes ranging from banana, apple and cinnamon and apple crumble to coconut and caramel.

inside information

Discover insider trade secrets to ensure that your tea is always as fresh and flavoursome as possible. Look at the best storage innovations to ensure the shelf life of your teas.

storing tea

Teas that are either vacuum-packed or stored in sealed tins have a shelf life of up to two years. Once opened, tea should be stored in an airtight glass container and kept in a dry, dark place, as bright sunlight and exposure to intense heat will both interfere with the quality and longevity of the tea. Also, make sure that tea is not stored alongside spices or strong-smelling foods, as the tea will eventually take on both their aroma and flavour. The Japanese often store their favoured green tea in the refrigerator, having made sure that it is well sealed in an airtight container. In this way, they are always assured that the tea they drink comes from fresh leaves. Once opened, black teas will last up to 12 months, whereas green and Oolong teas will last up to eight months if they are stored in ideal conditions.

safe-keeping

If blending your own teas from dried herbal ingredients and loose-leaf teas, store them in brown glass jars to protect them from light. Make sure the jars are labelled properly and always include the date on which the ingredients were blended, so you are not using items past their prime. Originally, tea was stored in a small container, known as a 'tea caddy', which held up to 500g (1lb) of tea. The name originated from the Chinese or Malayan word *catty*, meaning 'pound'. The first tea caddies were jars with lids made from terracotta, but as tea became a prized commodity, these were soon replaced with small, ornate chests with a lock and key to ensure the safe-keeping of tea leaves. As tea became more accessible, decorative tins became favourable, dispensing with the lock and key.

staying fresh

You can easily tell if your tea is past its best, as it will have lost its aroma and will create either a bitter- or dull-tasting cup. Also, if you find that the tea leaves a metallic taste after drinking, or if the water looks cloudy after brewing, these are sure signs that your tea is of a poor quality. To ensure that your tea is fresh and of good quality, buy a reputable brand. Price is a good indication of quality. Buy little and often, to ensure total freshness. If your tea is definitely past its prime, do not throw it out. Instead, brew it up, then use the leaves as a garden fertilizer. Cold, strong tea comes into its own to stain and age wood. Also, boiling up tea leaves in a pan will remove nasty culinary aromas that may be tainting the vessel. Bring the water and tea leaves to the boil, cover and simmer for 5 minutes. Rinse thoroughly.

selecting teas

Choose teas that are suited to the time of day you want to drink them, in order to enhance the way you feel at that particular time. For breakfast, drink Ceylon or English Breakfast. For a mid-morning break, opt for Rose Pouchong or Lapsang Souchong. After lunch, have a cup of peppermint or fennel tea to aid digestion. For a mid-afternoon pick-me-up, go for a cup of green tea, ginseng or ginger, Earl Grey, Darjeeling or Orange Pekoe. At bedtime, it is best to have a cup of chamomile, peppermint, Oolong or a lavender infusion. Tea connoisseurs highly recommend Assam tea with toasted tea cakes and Lapsang Souchong with cheese or salty foods. Jasmine tea is an ideal drink to serve with Chinese food, and fresh mint tea is a perfect accompaniment to spicy foods, because of its digestive properties.

tea types

There are six main types of tea, and all six originate from the tea plant *camellia sinensis*. The specific picking and processing methods determine the type of tea finally produced.

white tea

This is a more exclusive tea, as the unopen buds are picked from specially cultivated bushes in just a few days at the beginning of the season. The leaves are not fermented but instead left to wither naturally, then steamed. The pale, yellow tea they produce is low in caffeine and tastes mild and lightly sweet. Also known as 'silver needle', white tip should be served without milk.

green tea

Green tea is unfermented. The leaves are hand-picked then rolled and dried quickly so they do not go brown. Sencha is the purest variety as its leaves are rolled and steamed dry immediately after picking. Green tea has a distinctive aroma and a slightly bitter taste. To counter this bitterness, rinse the loose tea leaves thoroughly with water before infusing. Always serve without milk.

oolong tea

Chinese for 'black dragon', Oolong tea is semi-fermented, and the leaves are processed immediately after picking. The use of the whole tea leaf produces a pungent, fruity taste. Low in caffeine, this tea is smoother than black tea but less fresh-tasting than green tea. The two types, 'China Oolong' and 'Formosa Oolong', differ in taste due to their fermentation times.

black tea

Traditionally, the leaves were hand-picked, left to wither until limp enough to be rolled without splitting, then spread out in a cool, humid place to absorb oxygen before being fired. Modern methods create smaller tea particles, which brew quicker and are therefore used in mass-produced tea bags. Popular black teas are Assam, Ceylon, Darjeeling, Keemun and Lapsang Souchong.

scented tea

Oolong, green and black teas are mixed with different flowers and flavours to create scented teas. Well-known varieties include jasmine plum and jasmine, a mix of whole jasmine blooms and either green or black tea. Rose Pouchong blends rose petals with Oolong or black tea, whereas Earl Grey is blended from Indian and Chinese teas that have been flavoured with bergamot oil.

compressed tea

Tea used to be sold in bricks or blocks. The leaves were steamed and compressed together into solid masses, then left to dry. Modern tea bricks come in all shapes and sizes, and are created from tea dust that is compressed with hydraulical machinery. To use this type of tea, simply break off the equivalent of 1 teaspoon per cup, brew as normal and leave to infuse for 5 minutes.

what is needed for a flavoursome cup · tea pairings · making the perfect brew · brewing times

tea essentials

the perfect cuppa

Despite all the rituals associated with tea, most of us go into autopilot when making

a cup. We find a cup, fill the kettle, drop the tea bag into the cup, boil the water, pour

into the cup, add milk, stir and steep, before fishing out the bag. If you are after the

perfect cup, then you must create ideal conditions. Take the time to make tea and find

the utensils best suited to the job – you might enjoy the tea ritual as much as the tea.

Different types of teapots are suited to different teas. If brewing black teas, a stoneware teapot will bring out the full flavour. For stronger-tasting teas such as Ceylon and Assam, use pewter, cast-iron, terracotta or silver teapots. For lighter teas such as Darjeeling, Oolong and green teas, porcelain and fine china are most suitable. When investing in a teapot, ensure that there is always a hole in the lid, to fuel the tea with an air stream that prevents it from dribbling down the spout when pouring. Also, make sure the handle is easy to hold so you do not scald yourself. Never put a teapot in a dishwasher or in hot, soapy water. Instead, rinse the teapot with warm water and dry upside-down. To remove a build-up of tannin – which is an astringent chemical constituent of tea – from the inside of glass teapots, add 2 tablespoons of baking soda and boiling water to the vessel. Leave to soak overnight, then pour away and rinse with warm water. Never wash or clean the inside of an unglazed pot, but allow tea deposits to build up, which enhance the flavour of the tea brewed in the pot. Use separate teapots for brewing herbal infusions, strong, smoky teas or mild, subtle teas.

There is still much debate over the type of cup tea should be drunk from. The French would not dream of drinking tea from a mug, whereas the British are happy with a half-pint mug, and the Japanese use a rough-glazed cup without a handle. In the end, it is down to personal preference, but if you are looking for the ideal vessel, always opt for a rounder, more bulbous shape rather than a straight-sided cup.

bags versus loose leaves

tea bags Tea bags provide an easy option for a no-fuss, quick cup. No need to worry about using a tea strainer, or blocking the pipes or drains with obsolete loose tea leaves. Also, tea bags are a simpler solution for making tea in large quantities. New Yorker Thomas Sullivan unintentionally created the tea bag in 1908. The tea importer had filled small silk bags with tea to send to potential clients. The clients, instead of emptying the contents into a teapot, simply added the bags to the pot, welcoming the innovation. By the 1920s, the production of commercial tea bags was under way in North America. Silk was soon replaced by a gauze version, and consequently by paper. By the 1960s, the idea of the tea bag took off in the UK and business was booming. Today, in the UK, 85 per cent of the tea that is drunk comes from tea bags.

The production of tea bags has become an art form since they were introduced. They now come in every conceivable shape and size, ranging from square, round or pyramid to those that are heat-sealed, tagged or untagged. The materials used to create these weightless bags are Manila hemp, rayon and wood pulp, which do not affect the overall flavour of the tea. The size of the perforations must be sufficient to ensure that the leaves infuse properly.

While tea bags have a lot in their favour, tea connoisseurs maintain that they do not give as tasty a brew as an infusion of loose tea leaves. Often, the contents of a tea bag are of a lower quality grade tea, containing 20 different teas from four or more different countries, resulting in a stronger, more bitter taste. Also, tea bags often release too much tannin too quickly, creating a harsher taste.

loose-leaf Brewing loose leaves provides a more flavoursome tea and also takes you through the ritual. It allows you to experiment with different tea blends and sample new teas that are not readily available as tea bags. On a practical note, loose tea can be kept for up to one year, whereas the shelf life of tea bags once opened is four to six months.

The perfect compromise is to buy empty, large muslin or paper tea bags from specialist tea shops, fill them with your own loose-leaf tea and seal with a reusable stainless steel gadget. The bags provide sufficient room for the ingredients to unfurl and infuse properly.

tea versus coffee

When energy is flagging and you are feeling weary, a cup of tea will come to the rescue. Thanks to the caffeine it contains, tea is a refreshing pick-me-up. Although this mild stimulant has a bad reputation, caffeine is a natural compound found in over 60 species of plants and over 1000 non-prescription medicines. Chocolate and soft drinks, cold remedies and painkillers are all loaded with it.

caffeine content The average cup of tea contains substantially less caffeine than the average cup of coffee. All types of tea contain caffeine, but in different quantities. Black tea has the most, followed by Oolong and green teas. For a brew that looks and tastes similar to normal tea but is totally caffeine-free, try Rooibos tea from South Africa. Make sure you are not fooled into thinking that decaffeinated tea is entirely free of caffeine. Admittedly, most of the caffeine has been removed, but the average cup of 'decaf' tea still contains around 3mg of caffeine. If you want to knock caffeine on the head entirely, opt for herb teas, which are all caffeine-free, with the exception of the South American Mate and Guarana.

caffeine control In moderation, we can use caffeine to our advantage. Research has confirmed that 15 to 30 minutes after caffeine consumption, we will experience a surge of energy, although it is short-lived. Caffeine also increases the activity of our digestive juices, enhances performance, concentration as well as our sense of smell and taste.

Drinking coffee can make you feel anxious and agitated, whereas tea gives a long-lasting, subtle caffeine fix because the body absorbs caffeine from coffee more rapidly than tea. The polyphenols in tea slow down the rate of absorption. Remember though: your caffeine intake should not exceed 300mg per day (equivalent of 10 to 15 cups of tea). Long-term caffeine abuse can lead to mood swings, irritability and more serious health complaints such as high blood pressure, insomnia and headaches. It also depletes vital resources of vitamins and minerals, and excessive doses interfere with calcium absorption, a trigger for osteoporosis. Sudden withdrawal is no option though, as it leads to headaches, lethargy and irritability. Wean yourself off gradually. If you have high blood pressure, heart or kidney problems, it is best to steer clear of caffeine.

tea
solutions

water works Water plays a significant role in the taste of tea. Unfortunately, today tea is no longer brewed from fresh spring water. Instead, most of us use water drawn from the tap, which is tainted with chemicals that are not always destroyed when boiled. A fine film of scum often appears on the surface of a teacup due to calcium or bicarbonate ions in the water. For best results, use filtered water.

When boiling water is poured over tea, it releases a concentrate of extracts that create the taste, aroma and healing benefits of tea. To draw out the full flavour of tea, the water must have a high oxygen content. Always use water that has just boiled, and never allow the kettle to continue boiling, as this depletes the oxygen levels. Black and Oolong teas should be infused with just-boiled water, whereas white and green teas prefer boiled water that has been left to cool slightly.

If you live in a hard-water area, your kettle is probably prone to scale build-up. In order to minimize this, place a wire-mesh scale ball inside your kettle to attract scale away. Always empty out excess water from the kettle after boiling. If your kettle has a build-up of scale, choose a descaler that contains citric acid.

milky tea Milk embodies health, vitality, freshness and youth with its many healthy essentials. It became customary in the 17th century for the British to add milk to their tea. Yet, the idea did not take off in other cultures for some time. Adding milk to tea is really down to personal taste. Experts advocate that it is only appropriate with some teas as it spoils the flavour of others. White, green, Pouchong, Oolong, scented and China black teas are best drunk without milk, unlike Assam, Kenya, Ceylon and English Breakfast.

There is still great debate over when milk should be added to tea. It was originally poured first, to help protect teaware from cracking due to boiling water. Research shows that adding it first mixes the liquids better and prevents scalding the fat in the milk.

lemon tea Adding lemon, instead of milk, to black tea is a custom made popular by the French. Some critics maintain that it alters the taste and colour of tea, whereas others believe that it enhances the flavour of many black teas. The acidity of a slice of lemon will get rid of the bicarbonate ions found in water. Lemon marries well with Assam or Ceylon tea.

tea sweeteners

A tonic for the bereaved, a comfort for those in shock or an indulgence, tea sweetened with sugar makes an extremely tasty cup. However, tea was traditionally always drunk without sugar. It was only at the end of the 17th century that it became customary for the Europeans to add sugar. Tea connoisseurs maintain that adding sugar to tea tends to kill the flavour. If you have a sweet tooth and want to add sugar to tea, opt for a black tea or one that can tolerate a drop of milk. White, green, Oolong and China teas are best drunk without sugar.

sugar overload Apart from piling on the pounds and playing havoc with our teeth, sugar contains no nourishment at all. When we consume sugar or foods that are rich in sugar, it sends blood sugar levels soaring. The body reacts by using vital energy supplies in order to stabilize these high sugar levels. We may experience a sudden burst of energy, but this sugar fix is relatively short-lived, and after experiencing a sugar high, a plummet in energy swiftly follows. For all these reasons, it is best to cut back on your daily intake and gradually wean yourself off sugar.

sugar alternatives To replace sugar, avoid using chemically produced artificial sweeteners, as they are loaded with additives and preservatives. They are also of no benefit to the body, except that they are not laden with calories. Try using organic honey as a sugar substitute to sweeten tea, especially herb tea. Honey contains fewer calories than sugar, as it is made up of a high percentage of water. Honey also has some health benefits – it does contain vitamins and minerals and is reputed for its decongestant abilities. With tea, honey prompts the body to release saliva, which can help soothe a dry, sore throat.

Stevia is another alternative to sugar, and can be grown in the garden in the summer. The leaves are 30 times sweeter than sugar, yet ten leaves only contain one calorie. It can be bought in extract form and dropped into tea to sweeten. Also, liquorice root contains a substance that is 50 times sweeter than sugar. It is not recommended for pregnant women, those suffering from high blood pressure or heart or liver disorders, but it does assist with stomach upsets and ulcers. If you have a sweet tooth, look for teas that are naturally sweet, such as fruit teas.

tea pairings

Tea, just like wine, is more palatable with some foods than others. Although there are no set rules as to what you can and cannot serve with tea, many tea connoisseurs have tried and tested many combinations and come up with the perfect tea pairings.

suitable match

Opt for Ceylon, Assam, Kenya or Darjeeling teas if you are having a continental-style breakfast. If you are tucking into an English-style breakfast, you need a tea that is tolerant to fatty food, so drink Lapsang Souchong, Assam, African blends, Ceylon and Kenya teas. Try a China Keemun tea if you are eating toast and marmalade. A cup of green, jasmine, Oolong, Darjeeling, Ceylon or Lapsang Souchong will marry well with spicy foods. To accompany light savoury meals, opt for Yunnan or Lapsang Souchong. Earl Grey, jasmine, Kenya and Lapsang Souchong teas enhance the flavours of meat and poultry dishes. For fish dishes, Oolong, Earl Grey, Darjeeling, green and smoked teas are best. After meals, try sipping white, green or Oolong teas. Experts maintain that Lapsang Souchong and all other black teas go better with most liqueurs than coffee.

afternoon tea

All teas are suitable to serve for afternoon tea. Anna, the seventh Duchess of Bedford, thought up the idea of afternoon tea. When hunger pangs set in between light luncheons and evening meals, she instructed her maid to bring her a pot of tea and light refreshments. Welcoming the idea, she invited friends to join her, and soon the idea took off. This new trend lead to the creation of a wealth of ornate tea sets, equipment and silverwares. Also, many books were published, outlining the tea ritual and offering serving suggestions. Later, the word 'tea' became synonymous with a meal in its own right, and finger foods and fancies were overtaken by 'high tea', a substantial meal of savoury foods and sweet delights, eaten between 5 and 6pm by the working classes returning from a long day's work.

tea establishments

In the late 18th century, tea gardens thrived in the UK. Tea lovers could sip their chosen cup and enjoy the entertainment on offer in the parks and gardens. Tea shops also became popular throughout the country and today, tea shops around the globe are booming again.

the art of making tea

Master the art of making tea and you will produce the perfect cup. To achieve this result, always use good-quality loose tea leaves and a teapot suitable for the type of tea you are brewing.

prep work

Use the time it takes to make tea to relax and unwind. Turn tea making into a ritual and enjoy the experience. Always fill the kettle with freshly drawn cold water. Never re-boil water in the kettle as tea needs sufficient amounts of oxygen in order to infuse properly. If water is left to cool and then re-boiled, it will lose oxygen and make tea taste stale. Use a teapot that is suitably sized for the amount of cups you are making. When water is near boiling, pour a small amount into the teapot, place the lid on the pot, swill the water around to warm the pot, then pour the water away. You only need to warm china or earthenware pots – make sure you never warm a glass teapot. Some tea experts recommend warming the tea cups before pouring the tea, but it is time consuming and not really necessary.

brewing process

While the water is boiling, add the tea leaves to the pot – working on the basis of one teaspoon of loose tea or one tea bag per cup, although this depends on personal preference. Oolong tea is the exception and for the best results, allow two teaspoons per person when adding loose leaves to the teapot. To ensure freshness, tea should be stored in an airtight container in a cool, dry place away from damp and direct sunlight. If you are not using an electric kettle, do not allow the kettle to boil for too long, as it reduces the amount of oxygen in the water, which is vital for the perfect brew. Pour the boiling water into the teapot, stir and then place the lid on the teapot. You can also use a modern felt tea cosy to help retain the heat. Leave to steep for the required time, according to your chosen tea.

serving suggestions

While the tea is brewing, pour milk into the cups. There is still great debate over whether you should add milk before or after adding the tea. Traditionalists believe in pouring the milk first. Always allow tea to steep for the required time. If left for too long, tea can taste bitter and harsh, and if tea is not left to infuse sufficiently, it will lack flavour and taste insipid. When tea has brewed to its perfect strength and flavour, it was traditionally poured through a tea strainer into another warmed teapot, to avoid leaving the tea with the leaves for too long, which would create a bitter-tasting brew. For an easier alternative, pour tea into the cups through a strainer, then top the teapot up with some boiled water. Do not worry if you do not have a strainer as the leaves will eventually sink to the bottom of the cup.

sip and enjoy

Relax and take time out to drink your tea. Inhale the aroma, savour the taste and enjoy the overall experience. Use tea making time as a means to de-stress, put life in perspective and refocus. Look at tea as a tonic to salvage both the mind and body. Do not rush the ritual as you will only compromise the end result. Retreat to your favourite place to drink your tea. If you are alone, use this quiet time for mental respite. Relax, put your feet up and sip your tea slowly. To heighten the pleasure, indulge in cakes or biscuits with your cup of tea, or take tea with friends and loved ones. Most importantly, relish the moment. Time is at a premium in today's society, so take this precious time to reflect on life and remember: the past is history, tomorrow is a mystery and today is a gift – that is why it is called the present.

brewing times

Different teas require different brewing times. If left for too long, tea will taste bitter and harsh; and if it is underbrewed, it will be insipid and lack flavour. Get the timing right!

right timing

Most tea varieties will brew within 3 to 5 minutes, although there are exceptions. Depending on personal preference, allow Assam, Ceylon, Darjeeling, Earl Grey and Lapsang Souchong teas to steep for 3 to 5 minutes in order for them to infuse their full flavour and strength. Always make sure that you do not end up with a tea that is either overstewed or underbrewed.

the exceptions

Black tea that is made of broken leaves takes 3 minutes to brew, whereas whole-leaf black tea takes 5 minutes. Oolong tea brews in 7 minutes and green tea takes 1 to 2 minutes. Kenya tea creates a strong, brisk flavour in 2 to 4 minutes. China Oolong tea reaches its best flavour when it is left to steep for 5 to 7 minutes. You should leave compressed tea to steep for 5 minutes.

clock watching

If you do not want to stand and wait for your pot of tea to brew, but you still want to keep track of the time, some tea connoisseurs recommend using an egg timer instead of clock watching. If you are pushed for time, use a tea bag and squeeze the tea bag to speed up the brewing process. Tea experts might not recommend it, but you will still end up drinking a good-tasting cup.

bitter cup

If you have used too much loose tea in a pot, the chances are the tea will taste bitter and harsh. If you have steeped the tea for the recommended time, but it lacks flavour and is very bland, the tea is probably past its best. Do not throw it away though. Instead, pour the liquid into the garden and scatter the used tea leaves onto flowerbeds or herb gardens, as they will help condition the soil.

bland taste

If you do not allow tea to steep properly, you will never discover the true taste and flavour. If you remove the tea bag or loose leaves before the tea has steeped, it will taste insipid and bland. Any tea that has been brewed to perfection but has not been drunk can be used as a marinade for meats and dried fruits or used in cooking. Also, tea can be used to make sorbets or ice creams.

instant tea

This is the only tea that does not require time to steep. These granules of black tea, which are similar to instant coffee, do not create a particularly good-tasting brew and no tea enthusiast would even give them shelf space. To make instant tea, the tea leaves are infused, then removed from the liquid. The infusing liquid is treated to obtain a solid product, which is then dried.

herbal teas · healing infusions · medicinal brews · natural ingredients · making a herbal tisane

natural infusions

herbal
tisanes

Free from caffeine and full of goodness, herbal tisanes or teas are made from flowers,

leaves, roots, berries and seeds of edible plants. Not strictly a tea as they are not made

from the *camellia sinensis* tea plant, they make a tasty cup that is beneficial to health

and well-being. A herbal infusion may seem a poor excuse for your normal cup, but

once you break the habit and start experimenting, you will never look back.

Apart from satisfying the taste buds, herbal infusions are well-known for their healing properties. Herbalists work with different plant matter to create a medicinal infusion. Ask a qualified herbalist for advice or a professional diagnosis, and always buy dried herbs from a reputable supplier. Be aware that dried herbs are more potent than their fresh counterparts – powdered versions are even more concentrated.

When feeling under the weather, use your body's cravings to help treat yourself. When you are fraught and on overdrive, you will most likely crave chamomile tea and, when suffering from a cold, you may have a yearning for piping hot peppermint tea laced with soothing honey and lemon. When energy is at a low ebb, you may crave a ginger or ginseng infusion to put a spring back in your step. Try ginger and lemon grass to settle a troubled stomach and quell morning sickness. A mixture of cinnamon, ginger and lime leaf will ward off winter ailments and vanilla, cinnamon, lime leaf, turmeric and ginger will help cleanse toxic bodies. Milk thistle tea offers relief when feeling hung over, as it takes the pressure off the liver. Feverfew or willow bark are ideal for migraine sufferers and nettle tea will help those with hay fever.

When selecting your ingredients, bear in mind that some plants are poisonous, so only work with those you are familiar with, and always try to buy organic produce. Herb teas should be drunk without milk, but they can be laced with honey, lemon, lime or even orange juice in order to enhance the original flavour.

infusing utensils

There are various ways of creating a natural infusion and a plethora of different spoons, teapots and single cup gadgets to do the job. Admittedly, a bit more work is involved than simply popping a tea bag in a cup, but using fresh or dried leaves, flowers, berries and barks will create a much tastier brew.

tea infusers   Tea connoisseurs do not recommend one-cup infusers, maintaining that they do not provide sufficient room for ingredients to infuse properly, especially if you are using dried matter. Dried leaves will increase in volume when steeped in water. Look for a good-sized infuser, with sufficient perforations so ingredients can unfurl and infuse properly. For a no-fuss, no-mess single infusion, buy muslin tea bags and fill them with your chosen ingredients. Alternatively, infuser mugs, which are inspired from the Chinese covered brewing cup *guywan*, come with a removable infuser, which is a good size and lifts out of the cup. For the best results, always warm the cup beforehand.

Many teapots come with their own built-in infusers. The Cosiware teapot, popular during the 1930s and 1940s, has a removable built-in infuser in the neck of the pot and comes with an insulated chrome coating to help retain the heat. The advantage is that the infuser can be lifted out after sufficient brewing to ensure that the liquid does not stew. Glass teapots are ideal for making herbal infusions, especially if you are brewing flowers and buds, as they look wonderful. Glass retains heat, so there is no need to warm the pot, and it will not taint the flavour. Alternatively, invest in a cafetière or a plunger teapot and use it for making herbal infusions. Once the tea has brewed to the desired strength, simply use the plunger to isolate the ingredients from the hot water. If you are brewing dried herbs, you can top the pot or glass up with boiling water three times without jeopardizing the taste.

infuser aftercare   It is best to keep a separate pot or glass for brewing herbal teas, or the herbs will take on the flavours of drinks brewed in the pot. The leftover herbal ingredients or plant matter can be used as a soil conditioner outdoors. Simply rinse the teapot thoroughly with water. Wash every one to two months to remove stains from the herbs, but avoid using a harsh detergent.

healing
herbs

Herbs have been recognized for centuries for their healing ability. Medicinal brews may not be very flavoursome, as they often have an earthy taste and unappealing aroma. You can flavour them with honey, but it will interfere with their potency and healing ability. Do not expect immediate results though. Depending on your ailment, healing teas can take from three to six days to take effect, unless you are treating headaches, stomach aches or insomnia. Always consult a qualified herbalist if you are taking prescribed medication or suffering from chronic medical conditions.

the right choice
To relieve stress and anxiety, drink chamomile, lavender, St John's Wort, rosemary, skullcap and ginseng teas. Digestive, bowel and liver complaints are soothed with parsley, ginger, peppermint, thyme and dandelion. To ease both muscle fatigue and stiff joints, drink nettle tea. If your complexion is misbehaving, try teas blended from red clover, nettle and burdock, which purify your system from the inside out. For those with sluggish circulation, ginger and gingko tea will jump-start the body. To banish colds, drink sage, rose hip, garlic, ginger and spearmint teas. To relieve headaches, drink chamomile, feverfew, peppermint, skullcap and valerian. If you have problems sleeping, try chamomile, passionflower, skullcap, sage, lavender and peppermint.

making a medicinal infusion
To make a medicinal brew, use bottled water, not tap water. Even boiled tap water still contains chemicals, which can hinder the treatment properties of the herbs. Boil water in a glass or stainless steel pan, not aluminium. Work on the basis of 1 teaspoon of ingredients to 250ml (1 cup) of boiling water. Cover, steep for 3 to 5 minutes, strain and drink.

For berries, bark, roots, stems and twigs, make a decoction to release the essences and benefits from the harder, coarse plant matter. Chop or grind herbs. Soak plant matter that is too hard to chop overnight in water, then chop. Place 500ml (2 cups) of water with the herbs in a stainless steel or enamel pot. Bring to the boil, leave to simmer covered for 10 to 20 minutes, then strain. Add water to make the liquid back up to 500ml (2 cups). Always consult a qualified herbalist for exact quantities and doses.

herbal
advice

growing herbs Many herbs, even if they originate from afar, can be grown successfully either in the garden, in window boxes or in containers. When planting in containers, ensure that there is sufficient drainage. Basil, thyme and parsley grow well in window boxes, but rosemary, mint and sage require more space. Ensure that plants receive sufficient light and air to flourish. Containers will need watering daily during the summer, and feeding once a week. Replace plants and soil every year. If greenfly or aphids become a problem, use a harmless, organic insecticide or discard the plants and soil. When planting herbs in the garden, try not to disturb the rootball when removing plants from their pots. Using a trowel or hand fork, dig a hole that is slightly bigger than the pot, place the plant in it and fill with soil. Discarded tea leaves can be used as a natural fertilizer.

storing herbs Store fresh herbs in aerated polythene bags in the refrigerator. Large bunches of herbs that still have their roots intact should be placed in containers of cold water with a plastic bag inverted over the leaves. If you have grown your own herbs, you can freeze them while they are still fresh. For the best results, place individual leaves on a flat tray with sufficient space so they do not touch, or chop them finely and freeze in ice cube trays, without adding any water. To make tea, you can use the herbs frozen and simply add boiling water.

drying herbs To dry home-grown herbs, the leaves and flowers should be young, fresh and always picked on a dry day, early in the morning before the bees get to them. Handle carefully so you do not bruise the leaves. Either dry them in a very slow oven, in the sun or hang them in a warm, airy place, covered with muslin in order to keep the dust off. Another option is to place your herbs between sheets of absorbent kitchen paper and dry in a microwave for 5 to 10 seconds. Place a glass of water in the microwave at the same time to help preserve the herbs. When the herbs are dry, gently remove the flowers or leaves. Aim to keep them whole, without crushing, so their flavour is preserved. If stored in an airtight dark-coloured glass, wood or earthenware container away from direct light, dried herbs can last up to eight months.

natural
ingredients

peppermint
mentha piperita

In terms of flavour, there are two types of mint: peppermint and spearmint, which is commonly known as mint. Peppermint has a clean, sharp and menthol taste, whereas spearmint is warm and aromatic. Both are reputed for their digestive properties, although peppermint is more powerful. The high concentrate of volatile oils give the plant its strong odour, but also breath-freshening, tooth-whitening and decongestant properties.

recommended cup Peppermint tea helps ward off colds and flu, warms the body, relieves travel sickness and overeating. During the summer, drinking chilled peppermint tea is very refreshing and helps relieve nausea, headaches, heartburn and flatulence. Shred mint leaves, place them in ice cube trays, add water and freeze. Use these mint ice cubes in iced tea or other drinks when serving. Freeze peppermint tea laced with organic honey, to create a healthy alternative to ice lollies. Avoid drinking if pregnant or breastfeeding.

to grow This herb thrives in sun or partial shade in moist, nutrient-rich, alkaline soil. Do not plant too close to other plants and remove flowering stems to prevent cross-fertilization.

chamomile
chamaemelum nobile or *matricaria recutita*

There are three types of chamomile, but the perennial Roman chamomile (*chamaemelum nobile*) and the annual German chamomile (*matricaria recutita*) both yield flowers of similar aromatic and healing properties. These create a strong, relaxing digestive tea with a distinctive aroma. The other type of chamomile is non-flowering, and it is the flowers that contain the active constituents.

recommended cup Chamomile tea is great for easing stress, irritability, headaches, flagging appetite, colitis, muscle cramps, arthritis, rheumatism and upset stomachs, as it has an antispasmodic action. It is also very effective for relieving nausea, indigestion and morning sickness. At night, it will help calm overactive minds, prevent nightmares and help induce a peaceful night's sleep. Weak chamomile tea can be given to teething babies to soothe irritation.

to grow Chamomile thrives in full sun, in light, well-drained soil. Sow seeds in the spring and divide perennials in the spring or autumn. Pick the flowers only when they are fully open. Dry and store them away from direct light in an airtight container to use for tea.

rose
rosa

Fresh rose petals must be organic and unsprayed if they are to be used in tea. Apart from their appealing look in an infusion, they give a faint sweet taste and a soft flowery scent. Rose hips – the hard, bright fruits that appear when the petals are shed – are most favoured for tea. Their size and shape vary, and they have a fruity, slightly spicy taste. Rich in vitamin C, rose hips have blood-purifying and infection-fighting properties.

recommended cup A brew of fresh rose petals, rose hips, hibiscus flowers and honey makes a tasty cup. Rose hip tea helps ward off colds, infections, bladder and kidney problems and stress.

to grow Roses prefer a sunny spot and good-quality soil. Always cut the deadheads off roses to ensure they continue to blossom.

lemon balm
melissa officinalis

The delicately flavoured fresh leaves of this bushy perennial make a relaxing brew to treat headaches, indigestion, anxiety and nausea.

recommended cup Add six to eight lemon balm leaves to 250ml (1 cup) of boiled water, then enhance the flavour with freshly squeezed lemon or lime juice and honey.

to grow This herb prefers a sunny spot in a nutrient-rich, deep soil.

lavender
lavandula

There are over 28 species of lavender, all typified by a sweet balsamic scent. For years, lavender flowers have been used to scent rooms, calm fraught nerves and quell anxiety, and to enhance the flavour of ice creams, jams, sugars and stews. The tea brewed from these flowers is pale and delicately flavoured.

recommended cup Teas blended with lavender relax both the mind and body, and help promote a peaceful night's sleep. Limit your intake though, as excessive amounts can actually be stimulating. Lavender tea is an acquired taste, so add a few drops of lemon juice to make it more palatable. Blend equal quantities of dried lavender flowers, rose hips and chamomile to make a tasty, relaxing brew.

to grow Plant seeds in late summer in well-drained, lime soil, in a sunny spot. Collect flowers when in full bloom during the autumn. Dry, remove the flowerheads and keep in an airtight container.

ginger
zingiber officinalis

Ginger aids digestion, improves circulation and is a popular remedy for nausea, travel and morning sickness. It is also most beneficial for relieving stomach and menstrual cramps, hot flushes and also helps to flight colitis.

recommended cup At the onset of a cold or flu, drink a cup of hot ginger tea. It will help decongest a blocked nose and stimulate the liver to remove toxins from the bloodstream. Try adding a teaspoon of grated, fresh gingerroot, the juice of half a lemon and a teaspoon of honey to a glass of boiling water. Leave to steep for 5 minutes and drink. Also, try drinking ginger tea before and while travelling to ease symptoms of sickness. Sip ginger tea if you are suffering from morning sickness. If you cannot hold anything down, place a teaspoon of freshly grated gingerroot in a muslin square and fasten. Then, add to running water in the bath, and relax in the tub for 20 minutes.

to grow Ginger grows best in moist, nutrient-rich soil, in partial shade. It is the actual root that holds all the wonderful medicinal properties.

ginseng
panax ginseng

There are different types of ginseng, but the Chinese and Korean ginseng (*panax ginseng*) contains the most active ingredients. Ginseng has been recognized for centuries for its immune-boosting, energizing effect on the body. The roots and rhizomes (creeping roots) of this small thorny scrub proffer many healing benefits. The more established plants, which have roots that are up to six years old, are the most potent. The root is white when dried and red when steamed.

recommended cup Ginseng infusions are reputed to be beneficial for boosting energy and immunity, slowing the ageing process and helping us cope with stress. Try brewing 1 teaspoon of powdered ginseng root in a cup of boiling water. Leave to steep for 3 minutes and drink. It is important to limit your intake though, as excessive doses of ginseng can lead to hypertension, insomnia and nervousness. You should avoid ginseng if you are pregnant or breastfeeding. To make a brew, it is best to buy ginseng tea bags, granules, powdered or dried ginseng root from a herbalist.

jasmine
jasmine officinale

The flowers of this deciduous scrub have been used for centuries to perfume and flavour tea. They are reputed to have a calming effect on fraught nerves and overactive minds.

recommended cup To make jasmine tea, blend 1 heaped teaspoon of dried jasmine flowers with 250ml (1 cup) of boiling water. Also try using the blossoms of an unsprayed jasmine plant in a natural infusion. Jasmine mixes well with green tea and chamomile.

to grow This plant thrives in nutrient-rich, well-drained soil, in a sunny spot.

thyme
thymus vulgaris

With powerful antiseptic properties, thyme comes in a variety of aromatics, ranging from the traditional spicy-peppery common thyme to lemon, fruity or sweet thyme.

recommended cup Thyme tea helps alleviate coughs and breathing difficulties, and an infusion is great for gargling to soothe sore throats. Add a couple of fresh, pre-washed sprigs to 250ml (1 cup) of boiling water and allow to infuse for 5 minutes.

to grow This aromatic hardy perennial flourishes in light, well-drained, gravelly soil. It prefers to grow in full sun. All thyme varieties are attractive to bees.

nettles
urtica diorica

Most of us regard stinging nettles as a weed, but traditionally nettles were cooked like spinach and served as spring greens. Nettle tea is reputed for cleansing the blood, maintaining a radiant complexion, easing rheumatism and treating nervous eczema.

recommended cup Make nettle tea using 1 heaped teaspoon of dried nettle with 250ml (1 cup) of boiling water. It is a bland taste, so mix with chamomile or peppermint. To dry your own, pick nettles during spring or summer, wash and dry in a bunch of six to eight stems. Hang upside down where air can circulate between the stems. Once they have dried, cut and store. Fresh nettles can be frozen, but must not be thawed. To make tea, pour boiling water over the frozen leaves.

to grow Nettles thrive in moist, rich soil, in a sunny spot. Always wear gloves when picking to avoid the sting.

parsley
petroselinum crispum

Rich in vitamin A, C, B and iron, flat-leaf or curly parsley is a diuretic herb, traditionally used to treat fluid retention. It is also reputed for its effective cleansing properties. The berries, stems, leaves and roots of this herb offer its health benefits. The root is actually more powerful than the leaves.

recommended cup Drinking parsley tea after meals may prevent indigestion, and can be useful in treating urinary problems such as cystitis. Add a few sprigs of curly parsley to 250ml (1 cup) of boiling water and steep for 3 minutes. Avoid excessive consumption when pregnant or if suffering from kidney disease.

to grow Parsley flourishes indoors or outdoors, in sun or part-shade in rich, moist, well-drained alkaline soil.

rosemary
rosmarinus officinalis

This evergreen gives tea a refreshing pine scent and flavour, and is reputed to improve concentration and memory.

recommended cup Rosemary tea comes to the rescue to alleviate anxiety, tense nervous headaches and depression, to boost circulation and promote healthy skin and hair. Add a couple of freshly washed rosemary sprigs to 250ml (1 cup) of boiling water, leave to steep for 3 minutes and sip. Avoid drinking if you have high blood pressure, suffer from epilepsy, are pregnant or breastfeeding.

to grow Rosemary prefers well-drained sandy soil in a sunny, sheltered spot.

sage
salvia officinalis

Sage, a species of the mint family, is reputed to improve mental clarity and brainpower, relieve mental exhaustion, tension headaches, indigestion, sore throats and colds. This plant also has great antibacterial properties.

recommended cup Add a handful of fresh, chopped leaves or a teaspoon of dried sage to 250ml (1 cup) of boiling water, cover and steep for 10 minutes. Sweeten with honey to make this tea more appetizing. Red-leafed sage is preferable for treating sore throats and pineapple sage gives a fruity flavour to iced tea. Avoid if pregnant or breastfeeding.

to grow This perennial plant prefers a sheltered, partially sunny spot to thrive.

making a
fresh infusion

Follow these simple steps and get to grips with brewing home-grown fresh ingredients to make herbal tisanes. Freeze fresh herbs to ensure an all-year-round supply.

prep
work

If you are using fresh, home-grown herbs such as peppermint, sage, thyme or lemon balm, they should be picked just before use and rinsed thoroughly under cold water. If you are buying herbs, opt for organic varieties and wash them thoroughly. Before placing fresh herbs in a teapot or a cup, gently bruise the leaves between your fingertips in order to release the oils, which will allow the flavour to infuse with boiling water. Frozen herbs do not need to be thawed; simply pour boiling water over them. Do not worry if you are unable to find garden-fresh herbs. You can use dried herbs as an alternative, bearing in mind that they are twice as powerful as fresh herbs. Use filtered water when making a herbal infusion. If you are preparing a medicinal infusion, ensure that you use bottled water.

right
choices

If you are following a recipe and substituting dried herbs with fresh, you will need to use double the quantity of fresh, as dried herbs are much more concentrated than their fresh counterparts. When brewing herb teas, use a glass teapot. The infusing ingredients will look appealing and the glass will retain heat without tainting the flavour of the brew. There is no need to warm a glass teapot beforehand. Always make sure that you do not use the same pot to brew either black tea or coffee, as it will interfere with the flavour. Do not allow water to boil for too long, as it will destroy the vital oxygen levels. First add the dry ingredients to the teapot or cup, then the boiled water. Stir well and then leave the mixture to infuse. The infusing time will depend on the type of ingredients that are used.

brewing times

The aerial parts of herbs and soft leaves, flowers and stems will infuse more quickly than roots, berries and barks. On average, herbal tea made from leaves and flowers should stand for 3 to 5 minutes, and up to 15 minutes if it contains berries or roots. If you are using woody plant parts, it is advisable to make a decoction by simmering ingredients in a pan of boiled water to extract the flavour. Straining tea is not essential. Some plant matter will sink to the bottom of the cup whereas on the other hand, fresh ingredients are likely to float. In the end, to strain or not to strain is down to personal preference. After pouring your herbal infusion, you can top up the teapot with more boiled water and leave to stand. It should give you a second cup that is just as tasty as the first, but maybe not as strong.

finishing touches

When drinking herbal teas, take time to savour the taste and inhale the aroma. If you have concocted a brew from a selection of ingredients that look good, you should serve it in tea glasses or porcelain cups, and allow the ingredients to float around. To make tea easier to drink, invest in a metal or wooden tea straw, known as a *bombilla*, which derived from South American tea-drinking traditions. Another great serving suggestion is to add one leaf or petal to each cup. Herbal teas taste delicious, but if you are still unaccustomed to their flavour or find them rather insipid, try adding a small quantity of either honey or lemon juice. Moreover, a large number of herbal infusions can be added to a base of green tea in order to step up the health benefits and make an even tastier cup.

serving suggestions

If you find herbal teas insipid or uninspiring, use natural ingredients to enhance the flavour. Herbs, spices and other dried ingredients can be used to spice up teas and tisanes.

nutmeg

Sprinkling grated nutmeg into a cup of tea will provide the finishing touch and enhance the flavour at the same time. Buy nutmegs whole and grate them only as required, as the flavour from the seed of the nutmeg fruit evaporates quickly. It is best not to sprinkle ground nutmeg into a herbal cup, as it will look murky and unappealing. When grating into a brew, always apply sparingly.

star anise

To sweeten and spice up tea, serve with a crushed star anise. It will also sweeten your breath and add the distinctive flavour and aroma of liquorice. It is also a great flavour to add to apple tea. Star anise can be added to the teapot with other dried plant matter to infuse, then strained to serve. You can also float a star anise to serve. This fruit has been used for centuries to treat toothaches.

lime

For a refreshing, cleansing taste, add a squirt of fresh lime or lemon juice to your cup. Alternatively, scrape off the coloured part of the unwaxed peel, then grate and use in fresh blends. Try drying the peel and chop coarsely, or use crushed lime leaves to mix with dried blends. Use lime in small quantities, as lime becomes overpowering and can also leave an astringent flavour.

vanilla

If you have a sweet tooth, but do not want to use sugar, try vanilla extract. Create your own, by bruising or chopping dried vanilla beans and soaking them in inexpensive vodka until the vodka has absorbed the rich, sweet flavour. Strain before use and discard the beans. To add flavour, use dried, finely chopped vanilla beans in a herbal brew, or put a vanilla pod in any tea storage jar.

cinnamon

If you find herbal tea either insipid or uninteresting, try spicing it up by stirring it with a cinnamon stick. Alternatively, crush a cinnamon stick, place in the pot and allow to infuse with the other ingredients. Experts do not recommend using cinnamon powder, as the flavour is not as rich and fresh as that of crushed cinnamon sticks, and it will also create a murky-looking, overspiced cup.

cloves

Drop a few cloves into a herbal infusion to add warmth and flavour to a brew. Always buy cloves whole, then coarsely crush with a pestle and mortar before use. You can strain the tea before serving or you may prefer leaving the cloves to float in your cup. Cloves mix particularly well with orange and apple, but do not be heavy-handed, as the flavour can overtake the other tastes.

experiment and discover new tastes · create your own recipes · try blending your own teas

tisanes and tonics

making your
own blends

Experiment with tea and have fun doing so. Create your own tea blends and herbal

tonics, and discover new exciting tastes and flavours. There are no set rules as to what

you can and cannot do, and the good news is that you do not need to be an expert to

start blending your own brews. Provided you have a bit of imagination (or the right

advice) and good-quality ingredients, you can mix up dried tea blends or experiment with fresh produce. The experts suggest mixing up dried tea blends and, when brewing them up, you can add fresh ingredients to experiment with different flavours and tastes. If you are substituting fresh with dried ingredients in the tea recipes, make sure you half the quantities in order to achieve the same flavour and strength. Dried tea blends can be kept for up to twelve months if stored in airtight containers and in the right conditions.

Apart from satisfying your taste buds, tea can also be used to enhance the flavour of foods. In Japan, green tea is a staple of daily life, used to enhance the flavour of steaming fish and as a marinade for various foods. It is also used as a herb to flavour rice, noodles, stews and sweet dishes. To get more mileage from tea, try soaking dried fruit, sultanas, raisins and currants in cold tea before using them in fruit cakes, scones or tea breads. Why not add a small amount of jasmine, mango or rose tea to the syrup of a fresh fruit salad? Use cold Lapsang Souchong or Darjeeling teas as a marinade for meat or poultry. Another great idea for the summer months is to make tea-flavoured sorbet or ice cream. Experiment with mango, strawberry or passionfruit herb teas to satisfy the taste buds. Also, cold herb teas laced with honey can be frozen in plastic or tupperware containers, and then given to children as a much healthier alternative to ice lollies. Herb teas can also be frozen in ice cube trays and added sparingly to iced tea as a means of enhancing the existing flavour.

simple suggestions

Savour the taste and refresh your palate with these delicious, tasty concoctions. Whatever mood you are in or whichever season it may be, there is always a suitable tea remedy.

summer pick-me-up

Need a boost when the heat is on? Make up a jug of iced tea – not only will it help fuel you with much needed energy, it will also cool you down and refresh your palate.

what you need

8tsp Ceylon tea, brewed in 1l (4 cups)
  boiling water

500ml (2 cups) filtered water

freshly squeezed juice of 2 lemons
  and 4 oranges

1/2tsp root ginger (gingerroot), grated

sugar, to taste

lemon slices, to garnish

to make Make the tea as usual and strain. Add the water, fruit juice, ginger and sugar and leave to cool. Place in the refrigerator for at least an hour. Strain and serve with plenty of ice and a slice of lemon. Vary the flavour by using apple or peach juice, or try freshly made lemonade instead of lemon and orange juice. Serves 4.

relaxation remedy

When stress levels are high and you need to chill out and unwind, brew yourself this relaxing cup of tea, sit quietly and sip gently. Reputed to calm the nerves, this delicious tea will soothe an overactive mind. For instant relaxation, take a deep breath, counting to 6, and exhale slowly, counting to 10. Repeat ten times.

what you need

25g (1 cup) dried chamomile flowers

25g (1 cup) dried lemon verbena

honey, to sweeten

Mix the dry ingredients and store in an airtight glass container. Store away from light for up to one year. Makes 48 servings.

to make Add 1 heaped teaspoon of the blend to 250ml (1 cup) of boiling water. Leave the mixture to steep for 5 minutes. Strain and sweeten with honey to taste. This is a great drink to have at bedtime or when you are feeling a little nervous. Serves 1.

slumber cup

Having problems sleeping? Try drinking a cup of chamomile tea at bedtime or mix up this blend and drink it in the evenings. Containing hops, passionflower and chamomile, it will help prepare your body for sleep. An hour before bedtime, take to the bathtub and wallow in water infused with 6 drops of lavender essential oil. It will chill you out and prepare you for the land of nod.

what you need

500ml (2 cups) water

1tsp dried chamomile flowers

1/2tsp dried passionflower

1/2tsp dried hops flowers

1/2tsp orange rind, chopped

1tsp honey

to make   Boil the water then pour it over the flowers, orange rind and honey. Leave the mixture to infuse for 8 to 10 minutes. Strain and reheat if necessary. Drink in the evening or just before bedtime. Serves 2.

feel-good tea

At a low ebb? Need to give yourself a boost? Get yourself back on track with this tasty blend. It contains cooling peppermint and hibiscus and marshmallow root, which protects and soothes the stomach. The jasmine adds an exotic aroma and flavour. If you are feeling sluggish and unmotivated, go for a brisk walk. The fresh air will do you good and the physical activity will release feel-good hormones within the body.

what you need

10g (1/2 cup) green tea

5g (1/4 cup) jasmine flowers

5g (1/4 cup) marshmallow root, chopped

5g (1/4 cup) dried hibiscus flowers

5g (1/4 cup) dried peppermint leaves

Mix the ingredients and store in an airtight container in a dry, dark place. Makes 48 servings.

to make   Add 1 to 2 teaspoons of the blend to 250ml (1 cup) of boiling water, steep for 5 minutes. Strain if desired and drink. Serves 1.

winter cup

To keep winter chills at bay, try this spicy cinnamon tea. It is full of vitamin C and has a rich, pungent aroma. You can brew the recipe and reheat at will. During the winter, step up your vitamin C intake and try taking echinacea.

what you need

6 cloves

3 green cardamons

1 small cinnamon stick

500ml (2cups) water

3tsp chamomile flowers

60ml (1/4 cup) milk

sugar, to taste

to make Crush the cloves, cardamoms and cinnamon stick in a mortar and pestle, and place into a saucepan with the water. Bring to the boil, reduce the heat, add the chamomile flowers and simmer for 5 to 7 minutes. Add the milk and sugar to taste. Bring to the boil again. Strain and pour into cups. Drink while piping hot. Serves 4.

cleansing tonic

Need to detox? When you feel the need to purge yourself of the by-products of modern living, concoct this cleansing cup. Dandelion tea is a strong diuretic, but it is also rich in potassium, zinc, iron and silicon, which help replace any minerals lost through increased urination. Also, try a stint of dry skin brushing before bathing. Run a hard bristle brush over the body, making sure always to brush towards the heart. It will help boost circulation, shift internal waste matter and remove superfluous skin cells. Increase your intake of fresh fruits and vegetables, and take a 1000mg vitamin C supplement daily.

what you need

2–3tsp dried dandelion root, grated

250ml (1 cup) water

to make Place the dandelion root and the water in a pan and bring to the boil. Leave to simmer for 15 minutes, then strain. Try drinking three times a day. Serves 1.

monthly matters

Suffering from PMT? Try this tea to help ease fluid retention and relieve abdominal aches. If you suffer from stomach pains, fill a hot water bottle and place it on your stomach. Eat small, frequent meals high in starchy carbohydrates and low in fat to avoid cravings for sweet foods. Also step up your intake of foods that contain vitamin B6, such as meat, fish and whole grains. Cut down on salt and caffeine, and avoid alcohol as it can exaggerate mood swings.

what you need

1tsp chamomile flowers

1tsp dried lemon balm leaves

1tsp dried parsley leaf

1tsp dried burdock root

1l (4 cups) water

to make Place the dry ingredients with the water in a pan. Simmer for 5 minutes, strain and drink. Serves 4. Drink two to three cups each day before and during your period.

immune booster

When you feel under the weather, opt for this tea, as it is full of antioxidants, which will help strengthen your immune system and restore your general well-being. If you are a fan of green tea, you may want to try this one anyway. To help boost immunity and jump-start your body in the mornings, always finish your shower with a 30-second blast of cool water.

what you need

Two 15cm (6in) sprigs of fresh

   or 1tsp dried rosemary

1l (4 cups) boiling water

4tsp loose green tea

to make   Add the rosemary to a pan of boiling water. Simmer for 2 minutes. Remove from the heat and leave to cool for 2 minutes. Remove the rosemary, add the green tea and steep for 5 minutes. Strain if desired. Green tea can also be laced with fresh thyme, pineapple sage and lemon verbena. Serves 4.

cold decongestant

Suffering from a cold? Try a garlic infusion. It might not taste too good, but garlic is rich in infection-fighting goodies. Apart from helping to relieve colds and flu, garlic also strengthens blood vessels, reduces cholesterol levels and assists with circulation and digestive problems. To banish the smell of garlic, try chewing parsley. Garlic acts as a blood thinner, so avoid this tonic if you are taking anticoagulant drugs. Make sure to limit your intake, otherwise stomach upsets and indigestion may occur.

what you need

1 raw clove of garlic

250ml (1 cup) boiling water

to make Peel and crush the clove of garlic. Then steep the garlic in boiling water and leave overnight. Drink as a tonic in the morning. Alternatively, add the crushed garlic to the water and leave to steep for 5 minutes. Strain and drink. Serves 1.

beautifying blend

Radiant skin comes from within, but stress, hormonal imbalances and modern living can leave skin in a state of confusion and prone to breakouts, dryness or sensitivity. In Chinese medicine, herbs have been used for centuries to purify the blood and detoxify the body, which paves the way to clear skin. Many herbs stimulate the production of white blood cells, which boost our immune system and help it fight bacteria.

what you need

1tsp dried nettles

1tsp dandelion flowers

1tsp burdock leaves

lemon and honey, to taste

Blend the dry ingredients and store in an airtight container. Makes 3 servings.

to make Add 1 teaspoon of the dried mixture to 250ml (1 cup) of boiling water and steep for 5 minutes. Strain and flavour with honey and lemon. Serves 1.

morning-after cup

If you are suffering from the after-effects of too much alcohol, then get yourself back on track in an instant with this brew. Ginger eases nausea, dandelion root is a cleansing tonic for the liver and hibiscus is rich in vitamin C. Also, make sure you drink plenty of water to balance the effects of dehydration, and get some fresh air.

what you need

5g (1/4 cup) crystallized ginger, finely chopped

10g (1/2 cup) dandelion root

25g (1 cup) dried hibiscus flowers

honey, to taste

Combine together the dry ingredients and store in an airtight glass container, away from light. Makes 14 servings.

to make Pour 500ml (2 cups) of water and 2 teaspoons of the blend into a saucepan. Bring to the boil and then leave to simmer for about 20 minutes. Strain, reheat and serve with honey to taste. Serves 1.

refreshing tonic

If you need a refreshing drink to give you a boost and get your taste buds going, try making this fruity tea punch.

what you need

500ml (2 cups) water

5tsp Assam tea

50g (2oz) sugar

375ml (11/2 cups) freshly squeezed orange juice

1/2 lemon, sliced

1/2 orange, sliced

50g (2oz) strawberries, washed and sliced

to make Boil the water and pour over the tea, stir and infuse for 3 to 5 minutes. Stir again, then strain. Blend the liquid and sugar, stirring until the sugar dissolves. Add the orange juice and then leave to cool. Keep in the refrigerator. Before serving, add ice cubes and slices of lemon, orange and strawberries. To add a bit of a kick to your fruit cup, try adding 1 to 2 tablespoons of brandy or rum and honey to taste. Serves 4.

calming cup

Feeling stressed out and overwrought? Take time out to unwind and brew this relaxing tea – not only does it smell and taste wonderful, but it also calms you down and allows you to put things into perspective. To reap the benefits, sit down and rest your feet on a cushion while drinking.

what you need

1l (4 cups) water

2tsp green tea

10 to 12 fresh lemon verbena leaves, bruised
unsprayed petals from a medium-sized
  fragrant rose

honey (optional)

to make Boil the water and pour into a warmed teapot with the green tea, verbena leaves and rose petals. Leave to infuse for 5 minutes. Strain, then pour. Add honey if desired and float a rose petal in each glass for the finishing touch. You can replace lemon verbena with lemon grass or lemon balm. Serves 4.

headache relief

Suffering from a pounding head? Try massaging your temples with peppermint oil. Another option is to drink a brew made of six red peppercorns mixed to 250ml (1 cup) of just-boiled water. Leave to steep for 5 minutes and strain if necessary. Alternatively, make up the following blend and, at the onset of a headache, make yourself a brew.

what you need

5g (1/4 cup) skullcap

5g (1/4 cup) dried chamomile flowers

5g (1/4 cup) dried peppermint leaves

2.5g (1/8 cup) white willow bark

Mix the ingredients together and store them in an airtight glass container, away from direct light. Makes 32 servings.

to make Add 1 heaped teaspoon of the blend to 375ml (11/2 cups) of just-boiled water. Leave to steep for about 15 minutes, then strain and reheat if necessary. You should drink this brew while it is still warm. Serves 1.

energy booster

When your energy levels are flagging, jump-start both the mind and body with a cup of ginseng tea. It is also a good idea to go for a brisk walk and get some fresh air. The physical activity will boost your circulation and the fix of fresh air will recharge your batteries. Also, make sure you step up your intake of complex carbohydrates, and stay well clear of sugary foods that fuel the body with an instant but short-lived energy fix. Why not try a series of deep-breathing exercises? Inhale slowly through the nose and then exhale slowly through the mouth. Keep it controlled and calm. Repeat ten times. The surge of oxygen will revitalize the mind and body.

what you need

1tsp dried ginseng root

250ml (1 cup) water

to make Place the dried ginseng root and water in a pan. Bring to the boil and leave to simmer for 10 minutes. Strain and drink. Serves 1.

digestive ease

Do you always feel bloated after meals? Instead of finishing your meal with a coffee, choose peppermint tea. It will aid digestion and help refresh the palate.

what you need

2tsp mild green tea

a handful fresh spearmint or
   peppermint leaves

1tbsp honey

1l (4 cups) boiling water

fresh mint, to garnish

to make Add the green tea, fresh spearmint and honey to a warmed teapot. Fill the pot with the boiled water. Steep for 5 minutes. Strain, pour into small glasses and add a sprig of fresh mint to each glass. Serves 4. As an alternative serving suggestion, brew the tea and leave it to cool. Place a scoop of organic vanilla ice cream in a tall glass and pour the chilled tea over it. Serve immediately with a long spoon.

tea directory

tea stockists

United Kingdom

Kara Kara
Offers specialist organic green teas, including Pu-erh and roasted herb teas, and a selection of handmade Japanese teaware.
2a Pond Place, London SW3 6QJ
mail order: +44 (0)20 7591 0891

Neal's Yard Remedies
For herbal advice and mail-order service for buying dried herbs.
mail order: +44 (0)161 831 7875

The Tea House
Offers 45 varieties of tea from China, India and Japan, along with tea equipment, earthenware and tea paraphernalia.
15 Neal Street, London WC2H 9PU
tel: +44 (0)20 7240 7539

Twinings
Oldest teashop in London, founded in 1706. Sells a selection of fine-quality teas.
216 The Strand, London WC2 1AB
tel: +44 (0)20 7353 3511
mail order: +44 (0)870 241 3667
www.twinings.com

Whittard of Chelsea
Sells over 60 different varieties of high-quality teas in over 100 shops in the UK including compressed, organic, gunpowder and unusual flavoured teas.
tel: +44 (0)800 525092
www.whittard.com

Australia

Husk
Australian range of tea blends including tea tree and hawthorn berries and liquorice, peppermint and chamomile.
557 Malvern Road, Toorak, VIC 3142
tel: +61 (3) 9827 2700
www.husk.com.au

T2
Sells over 200 types of tea.
340 Brunswick Street, Fitzroy, VIC 3065
tel: +61 (3) 9417 3722

United States

In Pursuit of Tea
Informative website offering over 40 different teas ranging from white peony to oriental beauty Oolong tea, teawares and equipment, along with the history and origin of tea.
www.inpursuitoftea.com

Red Flower
Combining the rituals of the Japanese tea ceremony and the native South American tea customs, Red Flower's unusual organic herbal tea blends look inspiring and satisfy the taste buds. Tea should be drunk in a tea glass through Red Flower's ornate metal bombilla tea straw. '
13 Prince Street
New York, NY 10012
tel: +1 (212) 966 1994
www.redflowerworld.com

tea houses

United Kingdom

Claridges Hotel
Traditional setting for afternoon tea, which can be taken in the 1925 decor of the 'Reading room'.
54–55 Brook Street,
London W1A 2JQ
tel: +44 (0)20 7629 8860

Dim Tea
Modern café offering rare teas and dim sum. The owner will recommend which teas to have with your personalized dim sum.
3 Heath Street, London NW3 6TP
tel: 44 20 7435 0024

Mô
Authentic Moroccan-style café serving mint tea and selling trinkets and antiques from North Africa.
25 Heddon Street, London W1
tel: +44 (0)20 7434 4040

Savoy Hotel
If you want a traditional British afternoon tea with cucumber sandwiches, scones and jam and finger foods in a traditional setting, this is the place to go.

The Strand, London WC2R 0EU
tel: +44 (0)20 7836 4343

Australia

The Tea Centre of Sydney
Offers an exceptional selection of over 180 tea blends.
Shop 4R05
Glasshouse Shopping Centre
Pitt Street Mall, Sydney
NSW 2000
tel: +61 (2) 9223 9909

Vaucluse House Tea Room
Federation-style tea house set in beautiful garden surroundings.
Wentworth Road, Vaucluse
NSW 2030
tel: +61 (2) 9388 8188

Canada

T
Offers monthly demonstrations of the Japanese tea ritual and serves over 250 types of tea.
1568 West Broadway
Vancouver, BC
V6J 5K9
tel: +1 (604) 874 8320

United States

Hugo's Tea and Herb Room
Great place to have a brew or a herbal tisane.
8401 Santa Monica Boulevard
West Hollywood, California
tel: +1 (818) 761 8985

Japanese Tea House
Set amidst a Japanese tea garden in Golden Park Gate, you can sip jasmine, Oolong and green teas in true oriental fashion – even the waitresses are dressed in kimonos and tea is served from traditional Japanese wicker-handled teapots.
Golden Gate Park, San Francisco
tel: +1 (415) 668 0909

Wild Lily Tea Room
Tranquil, modern take on a Japanese-style tea room, complete with a fishpond. Choose from over 40 different brews of Chinese, Japanese and Indian teas to herbal tisanes. On the menu, the right foods are recommended to accompany different teas.
511 W 22nd St, New York 10011
tel: +1 (212) 691 2258

tea equipment

United Kingdom

David Mellor
Stocks a contemporary collection of teapots and tea equipment.
4 Sloane Square,
London SW1W 8EE
tel: +44 (0)20 7730 4259

Vessel
Stocks contemporary china and innovative teapots.
114 Kensington Park Road
London W11 2PW
tel: +44 (0)20 7727 8001
www.vesselgallery.com

Wedgwood
Offers traditional and contemporary teawares, including the range designed by Nick Munro.
tel: +44 (0)800 317 412
www.wedgwood.com

Australia

Chef's Warehouse
Stocks an excellent range of kitchenware.
252–254 Riley Street, Surry Hills
NSW 2010
tel: +61 (2) 9211 4555

The Essential Ingredient
Offers a comprehensive range of local and imported tea blends and equipment.
6 Australia Street, Camperdown
NSW 2050
tel: +61 (2) 9550 5477

United States

Takashimaya
Sells an array of traditional Japanese teapots and earthenware, and has a tea house-cum-restaurant in the store.
693 5th Avenue, New York 10022
tel: +1 (212) 350 0100

index

a

afternoon tea 51
    blends 33
ageing, premature 25, 70
Ancient Greeks 22
anxiety, herb teas for 62
arthritis 66
antioxidants 23, 25, 26, 87
Assam tea 29, 30, 35, 37
    brewing time 54

b

Bancha tea 30
bathing 26
beauty products 26
bergamot oil 37
bitter tea 55
black eye 26
black tea 23, 25, 30, 37
    brewing time 54
    caffeine in 44
bladder problems 69
bland taste 55
blended teas 29, 33
blends, making your own 82
blood pressure 25
bones, healthy 23
breakfast 30, 33, 35, 51
breastfeeding 26
breath freshener 66
brewing
    herbal teas 61
    process 52
    times 54

c

caffeine 16, 44
    in green tea 18
    in Oolong tea 36
    in white tea 36
camellia assamica 29
camellia sinensis 29, 36, 58
cancer 9, 25
    pancreatic 25
    prostate 25
Ceylon tea(s) 29, 30, 35
    brewing time 54
Ceylon tea 37
Ch'a Ching, Book of Tea 11
chamaemelum nobile 66
chamomile 66
    hair rinse 26
    and lemon balm tea (recipe)
        87

and lemon verbena tea (recipe)
    84
and peppermint tea (recipe) 90
tea 26, 35, 59, 62, 66, 85 (recipe)
cha-no-yu 12
China Oolong tea 36
    brewing time 54
Chinese ginseng 70
Chinese tea(s) 29, 30
    making 12
cholesterol 25
cinnamon 79
    tea (recipe) 86
circulation, herb teas to improve
    62, 70
cloves 79
coffee 44
colds, herb teas for 62, 66, 69, 70,
    74, 88
colitis 66, 70
complexion 26
    herb teas to improve 62, 73
compressed tea 15, 37
    brewing time 54
coughs 73
cups 41
cystitis 74

d

daily intake 23, 44
dandelion tea 62
    (recipe) 86
Darjeeling tea 29, 30, 35, 37
    brewing time 54
decaffeinated tea 44
decoction, making a 62
depression 74
demilikacay 15
digestive
    complaints, herb teas for 62,
        66, 70, 74, 91
    properties 35
Dimbula tea 29, 30
discolouration of teeth 25
diuretic herbal tea 86
drying herbs 65

e

Earl Grey tea 35, 37
    brewing time 54
eczema 26, 73
Egyptian tea making 15
English Breakfast tea 33, 35
eye tiredness 26

f

fennel tea 35
fermentation of tea 36
First World War 11
fish dishes 51
flatulence 66
flavonoids 25
flavoured teas 29, 33
flavouring food with tea 83
fluid retention 9
fluoride 25
Food and Drug Act 11
foods, tea with 35, 51
foot bath 26
foreign names for tea 16
Formosa Oolong 36
free radicals 25
fresh tea 35
fruity tea punch (recipe) 89

g

garden fertilizer 35
garlic infusion (recipe)
    88
Genmaicha (Japanese rice)
    30
ginger and dandelion tea (recipe)
    89
ginger tea 35, 59, 62, 70
ginseng tea 17, 26, 35, 59, 62, 70
    (recipe) 91
grades of tea 33
green tea 12, 19, 23, 25, 26, 29, 30,
    35, 36, 44
    brick tea 15, 37
    caffeine in 18
    and headache 18
    with jasmine (recipe) 85
    with rosemary (recipe) 87
    and skin care 26, 62
    and weight loss 19
growing
    chamomile 66
    ginger 70
    herbs 65
    jasmine 73
    lavender 69
    lemon balm 69
    nettles 73
    parsley 74
    peppermint 66
    rosemary 74
    sage 74
    tea 29
    thyme 73

Guarana herb tea 44
gums, healthy 23, 25
Gyokuro tea 30

h

hair care 26, 74
hangover 59, 89
hard water 47
harvest 29
hay fever 59
headaches 44
    and green tea 18
    herb teas for 62, 66, 90
health benefits 9, 11, 22
    see also specific complaints
healthy gums 23, 25
healthy teeth 23, 25
heart
    attack 9
    disease 25, 44
heartburn 66
herbal teas 58--66
    brewing 77
    freezing 83
    recipes 84-91
    serving suggestions
        77, 79
herbs
    drying 65
    growing 65
    storing 65
high blood pressure 44
high tea 51
honey 48
hot flushes 70
Houjicha 30
hypertension 17, 70

i

ice cream or sorbet 83
iced tea 19
    with orange juice (recipe) 84
immune system 25
Indian tea making 15
Indian teas 30
Indonesian teas 29
infusers 61
infusing the tea 53
infusion, making a 62, 76
injections 26
insomnia 44, 62, 66, 70, 85
insomnia, herb teas for 62
instant tea 55
Irish blends 33

j
Japanese tea ceremony 12
Japanese teas 29, 30
jasmine tea 23, 37, 73
jasminum 73

k
Keemun tea 30, 37
Kenya tea, brewing time 54
kidney problems 44, 69
Korean ginseng 70

l
Lapsang Souchong tea 35, 37
  brewing time 54
lavender tea 35, 62, 69
legends 18
lemon balm tea 69
lemon tea 47
lemon verbena tea (recipe) 90
lime 78
liquorice root 48
liver complaints, herb teas for 62
loose-leaf tea 43

m
making tea bags 43
marinades of tea 83
Matcha 12
Matcha Uji 30
Mate tea 15, 44
matricaria recutita 66
maximum daily intake 23, 44
meals, teas with 51
meat and poultry 51
medical infusion, making 62
menstrual cramps 70
mentha piperita 66
migraine 59
milk in tea 47, 53
mineral(s) 44
  content 23
morning sickness 59, 66, 70
Moroccan tea making 15
mugs 41
muscle fatigue, herb teas to
  improve 62

n
nasal congestion 26, 66, 70, 88
nausea 66, 70
nettle tea 62, 73

nettle, dandelion and burdock tea
  (recipe) 88
Nilgiri tea 29, 30
nutmeg 78
Nuwara Eliya tea 29, 30

o
Oolong tea 29, 30, 35, 36, 37
  caffeine in 44
  brewing time 54
Orange Pekoe tea 35
organic teas 30
osteoporosis 44
overeating 66
oxygen content of water 47, 52

p
PMT (pre-menstrual tension)
  87
panax gingseng 70
pancreatic cancer 25
parsley tea 62, 74
passionflower tea 62
peppermint 66
peppermint tea 26, 35, 59, 62, 66
  (recipe) 91
petroselinum crispum 74
Pouchong 30, 33
production 33
prostate cancer 25
psoriasis 26
Pu-erh tea 30

r
rationing tea 11
reading tea leaves 17
rheumatism 66, 73
Rooibos tea 44
Rose Pouchong 35, 37
rose tea 69
rosemary hair rinse 26
rosemary tea 62, 74
rosmarinus officinalis 74
Russian tea making 15

s
sage tea 62, 74
St John's Wort infusion 62
salvia officinalis 74
scale in kettle 47
scented tea 37
scum on tea 47

Second World War 11, 26
Sencha tea 30, 36
shelf life of tea 43
silver needle tea 36
size of tea leaves 33
skin care 26, 74, 88
skullcap infusion 62
smuggling tea 11
social class and tea 17
sorbet or ice cream 83
sore throat 73, 74
South American tea making
  15
Sri Lanka 29
  see also Ceylon
stale tea, using 35
star anise 78
stevia 48
stiff joints, herb teas to improve
  62
stomach ache 62
storage 34, 43, 52
storing herbs 65
stress, herb teas for 62, 66, 69,
  70, 84, 90
sugar alternatives 48
sweetened tea 48

t
tannin 41, 43
tassiology 17
tasting 33
tea
  bags 43
  black 23, 25, 30, 37, 44
  blends 29, 33
  break 16
  breakfast 30, 33, 51
  caddy 34
  ceremony, Japanese 12
  compressed 15, 37
  fannings 33
  green 12, 19, 23, 25, 26, 29, 30,
    35, 36, 44
  harvest 29
  iced 19, 84
  infusers 61
  leaves, reading 17
  making 43
  marinades 83
  Oolong 29, 30, 35, 36, 37,
    44
  organic 30
  plants 29
  rationing 11

ritual 8
scented 37
shops 51
smuggling 11
sorbet or ice cream 83
storage 34
tasting 33
white 29, 36
teapots 41, 61
teeth
  discolouration 25, 66
  healthy 23, 25
teething 66
thyme tea 62, 73
thymus vulgaris 73
Tibetan tea making 12, 15
time of day, tea to suit 35
tiredness 18
tooth decay 9
travel sickness 66, 70
tsampa 15
Turkish tea making 15

u
upset stomach 59, 66
urtica diorica 73
Uva tea 29, 30

v
valerian tea 62
vanilla 79
vitamin(s) 44
  content 23

w
warming the teapot
  52
wartime rationing 11
washing the teapot 41, 61
water
  filtered 47
  hard 47
weight loss and green tea
  19
white tea 29, 36
whole leaf tea 33
women's emancipation
  19

z
Zen religion 12
zingiber officinalis 70

acknowledgements

I would like to thank Catie Ziller for her on-going support and for giving me the opportunity to develop this concept. I couldn't have gone this far without you.

Special thanks to photographer Fleur Olby for her fantastic creativity and capturing the beauty of tea on film. Her calmness, laughter and attention to detail made this book a pleasure to create. Special thanks to Vanessa Courtier for her intuitive eye and great design, and to Carine Tracanelli for being a great editor.

Warmest thanks to the Sheltons for their insight into tea and its numerous uses. Thanks to my sister, Stewart, Lottie, mum and dad and to all my friends who always keep me smiling when I'm on the edge!

Special thanks to Susan Curtis at Neal's Yard Remedies for sharing her expertise, to Michael at Profile and to Yael and Victor at Red Flower for being such an inspiration.

Thanks to David Mellor for the loan of the tea equipment (pp. 18 and 19) and to Wedgwood for the loan of the Nick Munro teapot (p. 38).

I'd like to dedicate this book to my grandma who drinks more tea than anyone I know and who introduced me to the delights of afternoon tea.

First published in 2001 by Murdoch Books (UK) Ltd
ISBN 1 85391 999 3
A catalogue record for this book is available from the British Library.
Text copyright © Jane Campsie
Photography copyright © Fleur Olby

Project Editor: Carine Tracanelli
Designer: Vanessa Courtier
Design Assistant: Gina Hochstein
Photographer: Fleur Olby

CEO: Robert Oerton
Publisher: Catie Ziller
International Sales Director: Kevin Lagden
Production Manager: Lucy Byrne

Colour separation by Colourscan, Singapore
Printed by Toppan Printing Co., China

Murdoch Books (UK) Ltd
Ferry House, 51–57 Lacy Road,
Putney, London, SW15 1PR
Tel: +44 (0)20 8355 1480
Fax: +44 (0)20 8355 1499
Murdoch Books (UK) is a subsidiary
of Murdoch Magazines Pty Ltd.

Murdoch Books®
Pier 8/9, 23 Hickson Road
Millers Point, NSW 2000, Australia
Tel: +61 (0)2 8220 2000
Fax: +61 (0)2 8220 2558
Murdoch Books® is a trademark
of Murdoch Magazines Pty Ltd.